Anonymous

The Majuba Disaster

A story of highland heroism, told by the officers of the 92nd Regiment

Anonymous

The Majuba Disaster
A story of highland heroism, told by the officers of the 92nd Regiment

ISBN/EAN: 9783337193805

Printed in Europe, USA, Canada, Australia, Japan

Cover: Foto ©ninafisch / pixelio.de

More available books at **www.hansebooks.com**

THE MAJUBA DISASTER

A Story of Highland Heroism,

TOLD BY

OFFICERS OF THE 92nd REGIMENT.

EDITED BY

JAMES CROMB,

Author of "The Highland Brigade: Its Battles and its Heroes;"
"The Highlands and Highlanders of Scotland," &c., &c.

DUNDEE—JOHN LENG & CO.
EDINBURGH AND GLASGOW—JOHN MENZIES & CO.
LONDON—SIMPKIN, MARSHALL, HAMILTON, KENT, & CO., LD.

1391.

CONTENTS.

INTRODUCTION.

THE outstanding incident of the campaign in the Transvaal ten years ago (and which is forcibly brought back to our recollection by the recent visit of Joubert, the victorious general, to England) was the unfortunate disaster to British arms on Majuba Hill. It was an event which stung our national pride and galled our military spirit. It was easy to understand, after the first stun of defeat had left the vision clear, that a blunder had been committed, but it was not so easy to say by whom. The officer on whom had rested the responsibility of the movement was dead, and men hesitate to speak freely of the shortcomings of those who are no longer able to defend themselves; who have, indeed, paid with their life for the frailty of their judgment. In most accounts—official and otherwise—of the disaster, credit is given to the British officers and men for doing their best to uphold the honour of British arms; but in one, supported by the influence of illustrious authorship, this credit is taken away, and the British troops are charged with getting into what is rather slangily termed "a funk," and with "bolting" in face of the enemy. These charges, among others, are to be found in a passage interpolated in the "Cruise of the Bacchante," by Canon Dalton, who acted as editor for the young Princes of Wales, and he gives a narrative of the disaster which cannot be supported by known facts. It is as follows :—

"A funk became established among our men. The order to fix bayonets and charge down upon the advancing Boers was not executed. Weary and panic-stricken, the English turned and fled. Sir George Colley at the first rush was shot through the head. With a loud cry of fright and despair the English flung themselves over the edge of Majuba; the Boers poured on, and fired on them below as they ran like game. The Boers had one man killed and five wounded; the English, 92 killed, 134 wounded, and 59 prisoners. There have been cases when a defeat, invited by the mistake of a British general, has been saved by the courage of his men, but it was not so at Majuba; the men made no effort to turn the fortunes of the day. They commenced to run before the Boers reached the top of the hill. The reserves bolted almost before they had fired a shot."— *Vol. I., p. 369.*

In *The British Army*, by Sir Charles Dilke, at page 280, the author also says :—

"The one special example of panic which has forced itself unpleasantly upon the mind of the British nation in late years is the sudden flight of that small detachment of men which General Colley had led to the top of the Majuba Hill. The mischief on this occasion really was, no doubt, that the small force was not composed of complete battalions, but of detachments from various bodies."

Such statements as these might have been treated with dignified silence, or they might have been met with a direct denial. But probably a better way than either is to tell simply and plainly the true story of Majuba. It has never been fairly told. Gross misrepresentations have prevailed alike with regard to the action and the causes which led to defeat. The circumstances of the moment were not favourable for the accurate chronicling of events. The newspaper correspondents present were caught up in the whirl of disaster, and could do little more during the crisis than note the outstanding points. Those whose duty it was to furnish official details could tell all that was desired in a few pregnant sentences. For the rest, garbled statements have had to pass for facts. But the memory of the defeat has seated itself deeply in the minds of some of those who survived the engagement, and the desire that their honour and the honour of their corps should be vindicated induced officers of the 92nd Highlanders who were present to prepare some time ago the statements from which the details of this pamphlet are now drawn. The Majuba action is the most notable incident in the history of the regiment, and its Official Records state that " the grossest misrepresentation has prevailed about the details of the action itself, and the cause which led to its disastrous result."

Although not a third of the whole fighting force, the 92nd were more strongly represented than any of the other corps engaged, and their disposition was such that the narrative from their various points of view practically covers the whole ground. The documents from which the facts to follow are taken were obtained from the officers named by Colonel Forbes MacBean, who served for thirty years under the flag of the " Gay Gordons," and who had, some few years before the Majuba disaster, retired with the rank of Lieutenant-Colonel Commanding.

Feeling aggrieved at the obloquy attempted to be cast on his regiment, he has placed the statements at the disposal of the writer. The result is this pamphlet.

It may appear to some that the conduct of the 92nd Companies obtains undue prominence in the narrative to follow. But it has to be remembered that it is the officers of that corps who are defending themselves and their comrades against erroneous aspersions, that they tell simply what came under their own observation; and that it is open for other corps who feel aggrieved by the resented charges to take the same course. I have just to add here that my thanks are due to Colonel MacBean for the valuable assistance he has given me in refuting the allegations against his gallant Regiment.

JAS. CROMB.

January 1891.

THE MAJUBA DISASTER.

CHAPTER I.

The Boer Campaign.

IT will be remembered that on the 20th December 1880
the Boers, repudiating the annexation of the Transvaal
territory to the British Crown, threw down the gage of
battle. The Boers or Dutch colonists were hardy men,
admirable rifle shots, and possessed a quiet, dogged
courage, which gave them great advantage in the form
of warfare in which they engaged. In the Transvaal at
the time hostilities opened there were not sufficient
British troops to quell the Boer rising, and reinforcements were sent forward with all possible speed from
the Cape.

The Gordon Highlanders.

Among the reinforcements were the 92nd, Gordon
Highlanders, who reached Sir George Pomeroy Colley's
camp at Mount Prospect, on Wednesday, 23rd February
1881. The regiment numbered 629 of all ranks, and
was under the command of Lieutenant-Colonel G. H.
Parker. General Colley had already at Lang's Nek
suffered severely at the hands of the enemy, but with

this new instrument of war in his hand, a fair means was afforded of vindicating the supremacy of British arms. The 92nd was no collection of raw recruits, but a body of bronzed and war-stained veterans. They had fought with General Roberts at Charasiah and Cabul with a heroism which called forth the warmest praise from their victorious chief. Under Roberts they had accomplished the famous march from Cabul to crush Ayoub Khan at Candahar, during its progress exciting admiration by their fine physique, wide chest measurement, splendid muscular development, and great staying power. It was this body of men who joined General Colley at Mount Prospect, prepared to match their strength, courage, and skill against the Boer marksmen.

The Secret Parade.

Three nights after they joined the camp—on Saturday, 26th February—the order for action came. General Colley had resolved upon his course. What that course was he for the time kept to himself. Not a soul beyond the staff knew that any movement was impending. At eight o'clock orders were issued for troops to parade an hour and a half later with seventy rounds of ammunition, three days' rations, greatcoats, and blankets. The following were the troops called out :—Two companies of the 3-60th Regiment—140 rifles, under the command of Captain Smith ; two companies of the 58th Regiment—170 rifles, under Captain Morris ; three companies of the 92nd Highlanders—180 rifles, commanded by Major Hay ; and 64 men of the Naval Brigade, under the charge of Commander Romilly—a total force of 554 men. The troops mustered at the headquarters camp, and at ten o'clock marched off in silence—not a soul in the ranks as yet knowing anything of their destination. General Sir George Pomeroy Colley commanded in person.

Off for Majuba—A Perilous Ascent.

As the men tramped along, however, making as little noise as possible, it began to be understood that Majuba was "the end and aim of the night march." The men were heavily laden with their rations, ammunition, and other impedimenta, and when shortly after starting they left the level and began a winding climb up the side of the Umquelah Mountain, the march became extremely tiresome. At this point, about eleven o'clock, two companies of the 60th Rifles and one of the 92nd were detached to keep up communication with the camp; and then, leaving 200 men behind, the remaining 354 marched along a hill path on the right, towards Majuba.

At the base of this great mountain, which rises 6,500 feet above sea level, the serious work of the march began. The sides are rugged and precipitous, with great boulders here and there to obstruct progress, and at many points the men had to toil up the steep ascent hand-over-hand. Writing of the day after, when he accompanied a party of men up to bury the dead, Captain Forbes MacBean says :—" It was a fearful climb, and it is a perfect mystery to me how men with pouches full of ammunition, carrying rolled blankets and greatcoat, and three days' rations, could ever have got up in daylight, much less on a pitch-dark night." About one o'clock a company of the 92nd strayed on the hillside, and the other company had to wait a whole hour until the staff, which went in search of the lost men, were

able to bring them back. The sailors and 58th h
meantime gone on, and Lieutenant Wright, who w
inactive during the time the search for the mis u
company was proceeding, notes that the night wa
still that had the Boers been on the top of the hil l
movement would certainly have been detected from l
noise, slight as it was, made by the troops in ascend

The Position at the Top of Majuba.

The leading files of the 58th were the first to re
the top. This was about four o'clock in the morn
and the last of the 92nd got up about half-past f
When daylight permitted the position to be reconnoit
it was found to be "a plateau bounded by a steep bro
Here we quote the narrative in the Regimental Reco
of the 92nd Regiment, which was written by Capt
(now Majoi-General) Sir G. S. White, K.C.B.
"The position held against the enemy was a m
in circumference. From the centre and crest
this plateau the ground sloped downwards towai
the brow, so that the plateau was exposed to f
from the lower ground all round, but was especia
searched out from a ridge not included in the po
tion, but which was within easy rifle range of i
north-west angle. The approaches to the brow belc
were nearly all concealed from the view of the defende
on the top. The slope of the hill leading up to the bro
is broken by natural terraces which run nearly round tl
hill, and which afforded the enemy, under cover of h
firing parties placed for the purpose, opportunity
collecting in force on any point, and to circuit round tl
hill without coming under the fire or observation of th
defenders." In addition, it must be added that th

Boer camp, to command which was the only possible
reason for the movement, was beyond rifle range of the
position, and General Colley had neglected to take with
him mountain guns,* "which might," says Major the
Hon. J. S. Napier, who saw the action in progress, and
afterwards made a careful study of the ground, "have
been used from Majuba heights with good effect as a
covering fire to an infantry attack (on the Boer camp)
from below." It must also be stated that there was no
water to be found on the summit, and the spots marked
"wells" in the regimental sketch plan were, according to
Major (now General) Hay, merely a couple of holes dug
in the ground, when it was found that no water was to
be obtained.

The Disposition of the British Force.

A circuit of about a mile had to be manned by a force
numbering (roundly) 350 men, which was not homogene-
ous, but composed of detachments from three different
corps, and the members of which were exhausted by their
harassing night march. The necessity for extending the
men so much was due to the impossibility of observing an
enemy's approach, or determining at what point his
attack might be delivered. The defence was distributed
as follows, the Highlanders being placed by Major
Macgregor, who was on the General's staff:—To the
92nd were given the western brow and part of the
northern from 6 to 5 (as marked on the sketch) to
between 4 and 3. One company was extended, and the
other formed a support—not a reserve—behind the rocky

* In reference to this, Captain Forbes MacBean remarks :—" Taking guns to
the top would have been impossible. There was none with the force lighter
than nine-pounders of 8 cwt., two of which were in possession of the Naval
Brigade Detachment."

ridge marked 7, 8, and 9. The 58th held the eastern and part of the northern brow from 3 by 2 to 1, their second company being in support along with the company of the 92nd. The sailors extended from 1 to 10. Sixteen men were posted at 11, and a few at 5. Lieutenant Ian Macdonald held 6 with eighteen men, and Lieutenants Wright and Hamilton were in command of the extended line of Highlanders who held the brow.

A Short Time of Rest.

Instead of ordering the men to form such entrenchments as might have been possible in the time at his disposal before daylight, and before any Boer attack could have been made, General Colley ordered them to rest in their positions. He walked round the posts, saying to the troops :—" All I ask you is to hold this hill three days." Later on, when the hill was swept with the enemy's fire, and when no working party could live, he thought of entrenching, and, accompanied by Commander Romilly, went in search of a site. But it was too late then, and poor Romilly was shot dead by the General's side. The precious time had been wasted, and an unsheltered handful of men had to meet the concentrated fire of 2,000 marksmen, firing from perfect cover and from many carefully selected points of vantage.

Before the Battle.

" Shortly after 6 A.M., when just light," says Captain Wright in his statement, " a patrol of Boers went round the base of the hill, unsuspectingly, when a shot was fired at them from between points 3 and 1 in the plan—against orders, which were not to bring on an engagement if it could be avoided.* However, that shot told a tale, and the Boers galloped back to their camp with the news. Immediately all the camps were like wasps' nests disturbed, and it really was an imposing sight to see, that Sunday morning, all turn out, fires lighted for breakfast, and then a morning hymn sung ; after which all the waggons were inspanned, and the Boers turned out for battle. A storming party of about 200 men immediately rode under the second ridge. By crossing round under the naval brigade's position they could do it without being seen. There they left their horses, and climbed up right under the hill, where we could not see them without going to the very edge of the hill, and exposing ourselves entirely to the fire from the two ridges. In this position we remained till about twelve noon, the Boers climbing towards us step by step, and I may almost say unsuspected by any but Hamilton and myself, who could see them. Twice I went to the General and told him we couldn't hold our position with so few men if any serious attack were made. All he said was—' Hold the place three days.' "

The Battle.

The Records or "Digest of Services" of the 92nd, from which we have already quoted, gives the following account of the engagement, which we shall supplement by narratives from officers engaged :—
" General Schmidt, who commanded the Boers' attacking

---

* In reference to this statement, General Hay writes :—" When the shot in question was fired 1 thought it was contrary to orders, and at once started for the spot from which it had been fired. On my way there I met Sir George Colley coming away, and he told me he had given orders or permission for the firing. Captain Wright having received orders that there was to be no firing, would naturally imagine that the shot was fired against orders."

party that day, told Major Douglas and Captain Dick Cunyngham that he had 2,000 rifles employed in the attack. It thus became a question of time when the Boers would concentrate the fire of their covering parties, and deliver their attack on some point in the line which occupied the brow. Once in possession of the brow, they had but to lie down in the cover which it afforded, and search out the interior with their fire. At about 12.30 o'clock the enemy, having quietly completed all his preparations, fired a very heavy volley direct on the few men who were occupying the brow immediately opposite the ridge (on the western face), putting half of them *hors de combat*. The remainder ran back. By this time the supports had been greatly decreased by the call for reinforcements from different points, to keep down the fire and approach of the Boers, whose parties now nearly surrounded the hill. The few men left in support, chiefly sailors and 58th men, were now brought up towards the western face, but were halted short of the position from which our men had been driven. Finding that they could not shoot over the brow they were withdrawn, and formed behind ridge 7. 9. 4. The Boers then, led by a few Kaffirs, pushed in great force into the gap thus left in the western face, and there established took the north face in flank and reverse, and rendered it untenable. Almost immediately after the Boers showed in force on the N.E. angle on a Koppie, marked 2 in plan, which is the highest point on Majuba top. Our men now formed behind the ridge 7. 9. 4., fixed bayonets, and as the unequal fire contest could not be long doubtful, Lieutenant Hamilton suggested to Sir George Colley that the men should be ordered to charge. Sir George replied—'Not yet, wait till they cross the open, and then we will give them a volley and charge.' But the Boers were not likely to give up the advantages of their better positions and the superiority of their many rifles to cross the open and risk shock tactics with an enemy trained to close order fighting, and our men taken in front from the west, in flank and rear from 2 and from the hollow below 10 fell rapidly."

The Order to Retire.

" The ammunition, too, was getting low," continues the narrative in the " Records," "and the pouches of the men were being replenished from those of their dead comrades. At last the line broke. Lieutenant Hamilton, who was close to the General, heard him order the men to retire as best they could, but the ground was too precipitous for an orderly retreat, and all cohesion was lost. All those present state that before the last position was yielded the numbers must have been reduced to 60 or 70 fighting men, and there was a line of killed and wounded, chiefly 92nd, to mark the ground. Lieut. Macdonald, who held an important hillock (6 in plan) on the left of the position, had eight men killed out of twenty, and nearly all the rest wounded."

For seven long hours Macdonald, and those who survived with him, were exposed to the deadly fire of the enemy, until the very stones behind which they individually sought precarious shelter were " white with bullet marks."

CHAPTER II.

"ARE YOU READY, HARRY?"—GENERAL HAY'S NARRATIVE—
NOTHING TO CHARGE—WEAKNESS OF THE POSITION—
HOW THE FIGHT WAS LOST.

The Position Doggedly Contested.

FROM the narrative contained in the Regimental Records
of the Gordon Highlanders (just quoted) it is evident
that the fighting line did not break until Colley himself
gave the order to retire, and that it was the nature of
the ground as much as the Boer fire that broke up the
order of the men. Of course they ran—it was their
only chance of safety. But it was not "bolting," as
Canon Dalton suggests; it was not panic as Sir C.
Dilke asserts; and we shall find from the narrative
of Lieutenant (now Captain) Wright how reluctant the
officers and many of the men were to yield an inch of
ground, and how doggedly, during the severest of the
fire, they stuck to their duty.

"About one P.M.," says Lieutenant Wright, "we
saw some heads appearing over the top. The 92nd
rushed forward in a body and drove them for the
moment back—we lost about fifty killed and wounded.
Then, strange to say, the word to 'cease fire' came distinctly to where Hay and I were, and immediately after
'retire.' We all ran back to the ridge in the middle of
the hill, which allowed the Boers to gain the hill. Then
came the murder! In the meantime more Boers came

up, round where the Navy men were, and began to fire into the hospital, and so took us in rear. Hamilton and I both went to the General and asked to be allowed to charge."

"Wait," he said, "send a volley or two first; I will give the order!"

"Hamilton then said to me. 'Let's call on the 92nd, and charge on our own account. Are you ready, Harry?'"

"I answered 'Yes,' drew my sword and laid it beside me."

"We've got to die now."

"Macgregor (I think it was he) came up then and said, 'We've got to die now.'"

"Just then I heard the General say, 'Retire in as orderly a manner as you can,' when they all jumped up and ran to the rear. Hay and I and two men of ours remained where we were, all using rifles and firing our best.

"Macdonald still held his position and would not budge, neither would we. About a quarter of an hour or twenty minutes after the retirement, no firing had been going on from the rest of our troops, which neither Hay nor I could understand, as we thought by 'retiring' it was meant to hold the brow on the east side, where the 58th were posted.

"We were now being sorely pressed, hiding our bodies behind stones, and for another five minutes the unequal combat went on. Then Hay said, 'The battle's over; we can't fight a multitude; let's try and get away.'

"So off we four started in the direction which the

others had previously taken, under a most awful volley from the Boers on the Navy side and the ridge where we had been latterly firing at the enemy only twenty yards distant. Both the men were killed. Hay was shot in the leg and arm, and I was hit in the foot and turned head over heels. I had to crawl on my stomach a yard or two back to get my rifle, and so lost Hay, who got under cover somewhere."

"*A Charge would have been Madness.*"

We break up Lieutenant Wright's statement at this point, and leave the account of his subsequent adventures till a later stage. Meantime we turn to the narrative of Major (now Major-General) Hay, who was in command of the 92nd companies, for further details of the engagement proper.

His statement takes up *seriatim* the objectionable sentences in the "Bacchante" account of the battle, which he declares to be erroneous from beginning to end, and he refutes them one by one. He points out that what is called in official documents a "reserve" was no reserve, but merely a support, which, although originally consisting of three companies, had sent forward so many reinforcements to the fighting line that when the final attack was made there were only about twenty-four men left. He describes as "rubbish" the "Bacchante" statement that "the order to fix bayonets and charge down on the advancing Boers was not executed." Bayonets, he says, were fixed; but he supports the Records and Wright in declaring that no order was given to charge.

"Hamilton," he says, "asked Sir G. Colley to allow the men to charge, but Sir George refused to do so, and, in my opinion, was right in refusing. *There was nothing to charge.* There was not a Boer to be seen. From the position we then occupied the ground went down in a gentle slope for a short distance, and then came a steep descent. The Boers had collected just where the steep descent began, and without being seen themselves their fire swept the glacis-like slope which would have had to be crossed before they could be reached, and, besides, the slope was under a heavy fire from a ridge only four or five hundred yards off. A charge under such circumstances would, in my opinion, have been madness, and could have done no good."

In this opinion General Hay is supported by Major Macgregor, as will be seen by and by. The advisability of the attempt to charge is, we have reason to believe, still adhered to by Hamilton, but Wright, it will be observed, says nothing of the probable success of such a movement. Without, however, entering into the merits of this point of tactics, we emphasise the conclusion that the request of these officers to be allowed to charge, and the willingness of the men to follow, show how eager they were to grapple at close quarters with the foe.

Had to call on the Men twice to Retire.

Alluding to the " Bacchante" statement that, " weary and panic-stricken, the English turned and fled," the General bluntly pronounces it " mere rubbish."

" The line," he continues, " remained firing in the direction of the Boers till it received the order to retire. He (General Colley), I suppose, considered there was nothing to be gained by holding on any longer firing at an invisible enemy. His men were being shot down without being able to inflict any loss upon the enemy; it was a mere matter of time how long the unequal contest could last—simply depended on how long it would take to finish off the survivors. As soon as the ridge was left, and not till then, the Boers came on, firing as fast as they could. That the retreat became a flight is not to be wondered at, for the Boers were under cover on the ridge we had left, and we were crossing the open."

General Hay proceeds to characterise as " pure invention" the statement that the men uttered " a loud cry of fright."

" I was," he continues, "posting some men on the flank when the retirement began, and I did not know it had been commenced till I looked round behind me and saw that the line had gone. Even then a fire was being kept up by Wright and a few men posted behind some pieces of rock, and I had to call to them *twice* before they would come away."

The Boers did not Charge.

" There was nothing the men could do. They stood until they were ordered to retire. There were no reserves, and the supports did not bolt. We did certainly go before the Boers reached us, for the very simple reason that the Boers did not leave their cover till we had retired. I have met people who thought that the Boers had charged and driven us off the hill. Such is not the case. It was the crushing fire which compelled us to retire, and until we had retired not a Boer was to be seen."

Weakness of the Position.

Major Macgregor, as we have previously said, was on General Colley's staff, and his particular duty was to detail the men to their posts on the top of the hill. He had, therefore, special opportunities of judging of the nature of the position the British troops were to hold "for three days." He practically declares it to have been untenable.

"The defence of such a position as that of the Majuba Mountain," he says, "can be imagined when you understand that the sides most liable to attack were as thoroughly exposed to the fire of the enemy as the glacis of a fortress would be from the bottom without any more cover than individuals could collect for themselves in the shape of a few stones sufficient to cover their heads, and that not even the centre of the position was protected from the enemy's fire, as from the very commencement bullets were constantly striking the very centre of the position, and that not a dropping fire from a long range, but all from a few hundred yards distance."

Terrible Nature of the Boer Fire.

"The few casualties at the commencement were owing to the light fire of the enemy or the extended order of the defenders. As soon, however, as the Boers had made all their necessary dispositions, their fire was so overwhelming compared to that which could be delivered by the small number of the defenders (General Schmidt himself, who commanded the attack, having acknowledged to 2,000 rifles being levelled from the ridge on the Western and Northern slopes), that very soon after the heavy firing began there were few men on the Western and Northern slopes left unwounded, and there were not many, owing to the extended position occupied, left to reinforce and fill up the gaps. When the brow of the slope had to be given up, the next position was formed in a broken line, extending from the mound (4) to the hillock (6) behind the low ridge (9). If the fire at the commencment was searching, how much more so was it now, when the Boers were nearly surrounding the position—in fact, their fire extended from the northern almost to the southern side round by the western. The eastern, being higher than the centre, of course protected the defenders in the centre from fire from that flank. The line was exposed to fire from these three sides, and the men were dropping in all directions."

The Question of Charging.

Major Macgregor, as we stated, supports General Hay's view as to the impracticability of a charge.

"The order to fix bayonets was given," he says, "but the General could well see that a charge was impracticable when thus placed. In fact, unless the Boers had themselves charged up from some point it is difficult to see in what direction the charge was to have been made. I have been asked if a charge might not have had a moral effect on the enemy. I fail to see how a charge could have had any moral effect, made by a handful of men in a broken line on an unseen enemy, covered by a position (the ridge) from which an overwhelming and well-directed fire could have immediately been delivered on the defenders exposing themselves in an open situation."

The End of the Fight.

" General Colley," continues Major Macgregor, " seeing the small number of men remaining, and that these
few were being mown down without in any way being
able to silence the enemy's fire, gave the order for them
to retire as best they could. This they did on the
Eastern slope of the plateau, but part of the 58th, who
held that position, and who had also had their ranks by
this time terribly thinned, were unable any longer to
hold it. So it was with the few men left there, as well
as those who had retired from what I may call the
second position behind the low ridge (9) and mound (4).
The men, under Lieutenant Macdonald on the hillock (6)
(with the exception of one or two only being either
killed or wounded), were there surrounded, and either
killed or shot down.

How the Fight was Lost.

" It is imagined by many that the Boers actually
gained the plateau and drove the defenders off it, sending them back from each position. The Boers never
showed themselves at all if they could help it, and never
to such an extent as to allow a single effective volley to
be delivered at them. The defenders lost each position
from the few remaining men left to hold it being the
whole time under a well-directed fire, which they were
unable to return with any effect. It was like men in
the open exposed to the fire of an entrenched enemy ;
it was only a matter of time when they had so shot
down the men in the open that they could leave their
entrenchments without any chance of opposition."

CHAPTER III.

The Death of Colley.

Shortly after the order to retire was given by General Colley he was shot dead. It has been often stated that he was not seen to fall. Canon Dalton, however, in the "Bacchante" narrative, professes to single out the Boer who shot him, and tells how the Boer fell two years afterwards in the same way, the victim of a Kaffir bullet. Mr Froude, while believing that the truth can never be known on the subject, gives currency to the view that the bullet which killed the General did not come from a Boer rifle—in other words, that he fell by his own hand. There was little occasion for his taking his life with his own hand, standing, as he was, exposed to the fire of hundreds of Boer rifles, which had already dealt death to the majority of his men. No doubt, as he stood surveying the disaster, he must have felt that his military reputation was ruined, and his mind, already overpressed — perhaps unhinged — by the previous disasters at Lang's Nek and the Ingogo River, might not have for long been strong enough to resist the temptation to make certain that he would not live to face inevitable censure and ignominy. But he *was* saved the degradation of suicide.

His death was almost a murder. Captain Morris, of the 58th, saw the deed done. The Captain was lying severely wounded a short distance from where the General was standing. The General's head was uncovered, and he was waving a white handkerchief—doubtless meant as a sign of truce. He was alone, for as Wright says—" General Colley never went himself when he said retire." A young Boer, a mere boy, approached him, and when within a few yards took deliberate aim and shot him through the head. " The bullet," says Wright, " went in at his right side, just over the eye, and made an enormous hole at the back of his head."

How Disaster might have been Averted.

It is an open question whether the day might have been saved at all. Had the occupation of Majuba been part of a larger scheme—had it been a feint to draw off the attention of the Boers while an attack from Mount Prospect was being pushed forward against the Boer encampment at Lang's Nek, the defenders of the position might have been able to hold on as long as required. But whatever Colley's intentions may have been, the movement resolved itself into an isolated project; for no concerted action was arranged with the officers left behind in command of the British troops—they did not even know the destination or object of the expedition— and the General had actually separated himself from the companies left to maintain communication, and even from his reserve ammunition. He thus left himself no possible chance of success.

In regard to this point Major-General Hay says :—
" The only thing that could have saved the day would
have been an attack on the Nek from Mount Prospect.
But Colley had kept the officer in command there entirely
without instructions. I believe he intended to go back
himself, but did not do so."

The evidence that the unfortunate General intended
to go back is conclusive ; but it betrays a lamentable
degree of indecision and want of skill. In answer to an
inquiry as to his grounds for belief that Colley intended
to return to Mount Prospect, General Hay writes :—
" He had sent to Newcastle for the 60th and the 15th
Hussars, and it was understood that he intended to
attack Lang's Nek on the following morning from Mount
Prospect, while the Majuba detachment acted on the
flank. The fact was, either he was a day late in sending
for the Hussars and 60th, or he moved on to Mount
Prospect a day too soon. He told me himself that he
intended to return to camp ' soon,' and that he would
send up more ammunition and men—in fact, reinforce
us. Essex was staff officer to the Colonel left in command
of the camp, and I am sure he will bear me out in saying
that they were left without orders of any kind. Herbert
Stewart (since killed in the Soudan) also told me that
Colley was going back to camp as soon as he had made
some arrangements about the troops on Majuba."

Alluding to the possibility of the movement being
successful, Major Macgregor adopts the same view as
General Hay—

" In my humble opinion," he says, " the only way to
have saved the disaster on Majuba was by an attack to
have been made from Mount Prospect as soon as it was
found the position was so faulty. The Boers must have
then either relinquished the attack on Majuba or lost

Lang's Nek. But seeing no move being made from the camp at Mount Prospect, they sent every available man to attack Majuba. As Majuba was in signalling communication with Mount Prospect, all orders for the attack could have been communicated by General Colley to the officer commanding at the camp." But the General neither communicated with nor returned to the camp, and so all chance of success was lost.

A Sinister Rumour.

The question may be asked why General Colley made this precipitate and venturesome march to Majuba. The circumstances in which he found himself must be taken into consideration in answering this question. General Colley had twice smarted under the fire of the Boers. At Lang's Nek he was repulsed, with seven officers and eighty men killed and a hundred wounded; and at the Ingogo River he lost six officers and sixty-four men, besides sixty-four wounded. Meanwhile reinforcements were hurrying forward from home and from India. Sir Evelyn Wood was also in the neighbourhood, and it was whispered that he was about to patch up peace with the Boers. May not Sir George Colley have wished to retrieve his good name by a successful brush with the Boers before the reinforcements arrived, and before Sir Evelyn Wood had made peace with the enemy?

A report current in the camp gives foundation to this belief. A lady, very closely related to Sir George Colley, was at Newcastle, a town a few miles distant from the camp. After General Colley's death it is stated, upon authority that need not be questioned, that a letter from this lady was found on his body to the effect that Colley now had his opportunity (General Wood being absent), and that if he did not do something she would "never speak to him again." Poor Colley; he did something, and she never had opportunity to speak to him again.

After the Battle—Flag of Truce Fired on.

We now recur to the statement of Lieutenant Wright, which was broken off at the stage when, unable longer to maintain the unequal combat, he turned with Major Hay to follow the already broken line. The two men by whom the officers were accompanied were killed, and both officers were wounded.

" I got down the hill a bit," says Lieutenant Wright, "when a man said from some thick bushes, ' I say, Wright, have you a handkerchief ? '

"Thinking the man was wounded, I said, ' Yes, can I do anything for you ? '

" ' Oh ! ' he replied, ' I'm not wounded, but put it on your bayonet as a flag of truce.' I politely told him to go to the devil, and that I meant going home.

" All this time there was a scattering fire from the Boers.

" Another fifty yards, and I heard another voice— ' For Heaven's sake ! help me here with these men.'

" This time it was Macgregor, who was in some bushes with several men who were wounded by the firing while in hiding. I went in, and Macgregor said, ' Go out with your handkerchief and wave it as a sign we've had enough of this carnage."

" So I put it on my bayonet and went out, but immediately they fired at me, and one bullet went through the stock of the rifle and must have killed me otherwise."

"So I went in again and said, 'I go out for no one again,' stuck the gun on a bush with the flag up, and then got behind a stone.

"The Boers still fired, so I told Smith, the Colonel's servant, that he might like to try conciliation with the flag. But he didn't see it, so we lay where we were till the firing stopped. Then the Boers came down and said they would not hurt us if we came out. So out we went. They immediately rushed at us and began dragging our belts off.

'Why do you Fight us on Sunday?'

"The first thing they said to me was, 'Why do you fight us on Sunday?'

"'I don't care whether it's Sunday or Monday,' I replied. 'I don't want to fight you at all; but I just do as I am told.'

"The fellow then wanted my watch, which I would not give him. He said it was for Joubert. I said I would give Joubert the watch when he asked for it. Eventually he got it. Going through a thicket of castor oil plants, he placed his rifle to my ear, and told me to deliver it while he counted ten or die. I gave up the watch.

"Macgregor and I then asked to be allowed to go and help our wounded. They let him go, but would not let me. They said I would escape. Staunton was with the company left below, and didn't go up the hill. When their laager was attacked, he, in escaping, fell into a clump of trees, and lay still with two men also there.

The men unfortunately began talking, when the Boers heard them, and took him too. Hamilton was shot in the main retreat. He lay down to have a last shot, and was hit by a bullet in the wrist while aiming. After that we were marched off by the Boers."

These gallant officers subsequently gained their liberty.

CHAPTER IV.

BURYING THE DEAD—A HORRID SIGHT—THE MEN SHOT IN THE HEAD—SPORRANS AS TROPHIES OF WAR—THE HONOURS OF THE FIGHT.

Captain MacBean's Statement.

THE British were defeated ; massacred, if you will. They would have been annihilated had they stayed on the hill long enough exposed to that terrible fire. Their dead and wounded were left behind. Next day a party was sent out from the camp at Mount Prospect to give what help was possible to the wounded, and to perform the last meagre, melancholy offices to the dead. With this party, which numbered about a hundred men, was Captain Forbes MacBean, 92nd Regiment. As this gallant officer's statement, besides vividly describing the scene on Majuba after the battle, gives a clear idea of the situation as viewed from Mount Prospect after the

Majuba expedition had left the camp, we give it as written :—

"On the night of 26th February 1881, at about 10 P.M.," he says, " I proceeded on outlying piquet from Mount Prospect, to relieve Lieutenant Hamilton of my regiment, whose company had paraded at the head quarters camp a little time before. At daybreak the following morning (Sunday) one or two men (one was a signaller) came to where I was, and we tried to discover the whereabouts of the men who had left camp the previous night. We looked in every direction, and at last the signaller discovered them on the top of a plateau, some three miles from camp, in the direction, and rather to the left or west, of Lang's Nek. With field glasses it could be seen that they were moving about, apparently two or three men at a time, but, although the morning was clear, distance prevented their being visible except when against the sky line. I was relieved off piquet about 8 A.M. Soon we heard firing (as far as I can remember this must have been about 9 A.M.) ; we could see the smoke from the volleys distinctly, and I have a vivid recollection of our laughing as we sat in our mess tent and saying we wished we were up there potting 'Pinheads' as they came up the hill."

" About ten o'clock, Mr Ritchie, the English minister, came across from his tent at headquarters and sat with us. He said he was much afraid of the result of Sir G. Colley's adventure, and appeared very nervous and out of spirits. We all thought he knew more about it than he cared to say. At about 12.30 the men in camp were suddenly ordered to turn out. We fell in and marched to the part of the camp where the hospital, 60th, and headquarter tents were—that is, the side next

Majuba. We extended, and the men lay down. All this time there was heavy firing on the top of the hill. After waiting on the Veldt for about twenty minutes, the firing got more slack, and to our surprise we saw three men coming towards us from the direction of Majuba. They were about half a mile away, and walking very slowly. I and one or two others ran towards them, and we saw it was three of our own men (92nd), the centre one wounded, supported by the others, and all terribly exhausted.

"I asked them who were on the top of the hill.

"To our amazement they answered 'The Dutch.'

"They then told us how they had been driven off, but they were so done up they could scarcely talk. Other men of other regiments then began to appear, and Fitzroy Hay, a correspondent, among them. The force which had been left on the ridge connecting Umquelah and Majuba (to keep open communication with the camp) had been driven in by a large force of Boers ; but the field guns with us checked them, and prevented them following up their success. With few exceptions, all the men who returned to camp were wounded."

The Dead—where and how they were found.

"Next morning at daylight," continues Captain MacBean, "I was ordered to parade with a party of men and proceed to headquarters camp. On arriving there we were joined by a party of bluejackets and 58th men. The whole numbered about 100, and was under command of a naval officer whose name I forget, but who was given a note to give to Joubert, and was supplied with a white flag. We started off, via O'Neill's farm, towards the top of the ridge where the connecting party had been left the previous night.

"At the foot of the slope we were stopped by a Boer vidette, who in English asked what we wanted. He was given the note, and told to take it to Kruger or Joubert, which he did. We were then allowed to ascend the ridge, looking for dead bodies on our way, but found none. We then marched towards Majuba to collect and bury the dead. It was a fearful climb, and it is a perfect mystery to me how men with pouches full of ammunition, carrying rolled blanket and greatcoat, and three days' rations, could ever have got up in daylight, much less on a pitch-dark night. We passed seven or eight bodies on the way up, but left them to be buried after the heavy work on the top was got through."

A Horrid Sight.

"The top of Majuba was a horrid sight. The first thing I saw was a long row of dead men—some forty or fifty of them. There were also numbers of wounded men lying about—some on the ground, others on stretchers—most of them frightfully wounded. I went towards the edge of the hill, where so many of the 92nd men had been killed. There the grass was a mass of blood and brains, and was red all over. There were a lot of Boers up there, but of course we took no notice of them, and they gradually left. The men set to work to dig the grave. This took some time, so I had plenty of leisure to look round. There was lots to do, helping and giving water to the wounded men. There were not many of them left, as most had been taken to O'Neill's farm. Only the worst cases had been left on the hill as they were dying, and it would not have been worth while carrying them all the way down, and would only have caused them much pain and killed them sooner."

The Fatal Ridge.

" The chief thing that struck us was the great size of the top of the hill—from the camp it looked very different—and it was easy to see how the men had been killed off when lying on the brow on the N.W. side, as it was swept by fire from another hill some 600 or 700 yards away."

Where the Bullets Lodged.

" The dead were all shot above the chest ; in some men's heads I counted five and six bullet wounds. Helmets were riddled. Lieutenant Wright, of my regiment, had two bullets through his helmet—one making an extra parting of his hair without cutting the skin. He was the last off the hill ; he wouldn't leave. Major Hay had to order him off, and Wright kept begging to be allowed to stay and have another shot.

" Eventually the grave was dug, and the men put in in three layers, some Boers helping us. To the best of my recollection, we put about seventy-five bodies in. Before it was done a heavy mist and rain came on.

" We then went about 200 yards down the hill, and collected fourteen more bodies—-chiefly 92nd men—and buried them there. Five or six of them had been alive and trying to get into camp when we went up in the morning, but they had soon after died—so the men who

had been left with them told us. We then marched
home in tremendous rain, the men all very tired and
down-hearted." Little need to wonder at their
despondency.

Appearance of the Boers.

" I had ample time and opportunity during my sad
task of studying the appearance of the Boers, and, to
speak generally, should say that, take an ordinary
specimen, and you have a dirty, unkempt-looking fellow,
with long hair and beard, very much tanned, his face
the colour of mahogany, generally a broad-shouldered,
hard-looking man, his dress of all sorts and conditions—
usually a coat that will just hold together, and a pair of
baggy corduroy trousers. The chances are he has one
spur on upside down, his head covered with a broad-
brimmed felt hat, high in the crown, and a dirty flannel
shirt ; his rifle, generally a repeating Winchester, the
cartridges carried *en bandolier.*"

Sporrans as Trophies.

" The Boers would not let us take anything from the
bodies of those who had fallen. They took all the rifles
and belts, but what they seemed to prize most were the
poor fellows' sporrans, and I was afterwards told by a
man, who had been in their country, that these trophies
of victory had the place of honour in their houses.

" They were naturally much elated, and many of them
inclined to be impertinent. As soon as they had
identified the General's body they took it down to their

camp, from which it was afterwards brought to Mount Prospect, and buried in the cemetery there."

The 92nd Casualty List.

The 92nd suffered by far the most heavily. Of twenty men holding the disputed hillock under Lieutenant Macdonald, eight, as we have already said, were killed, and nearly all the rest wounded. But it was along the slope facing the direct attack where the carnage was greatest, and this was held by the 92nd. Scarcely a man escaped. One hundred and twenty had gone into action, and only 24 came out unscathed—33 being killed and 63 wounded, most of them seriously. Poor fellows, there were few of them left either to run or "funk." Their wounds tell how bravely they faced the fire.

How the Officers Behaved.

The statements already given, confirming each other at almost every point, will have shown the reader that the officers present behaved according to the best traditions of their class in the British service. They stood by their men, and firing themselves, encouraged them as long as it was prudent, and, in some cases, after it was positively suicidal, to keep up the unequal combat.

The 92nd "Record," from which we have already quoted, bears emphatic and dignified testimony to this. "That everything," it says, "that lay within the power of regimental officers towards turning the result of the action was done the names of the officers of the 92nd

Highlanders who took part in the day's proceedings is the best guarantee, and we have the testimony of the highest authorities in the despatches from which quotations are given. The officers were—Major Hay (severely wounded), Captain Singleton (died of his wounds), Captain Macgregor, Lieutenant Hamilton (severely wounded), Lieutenants Wright and Macdonald."

Whose was the Blunder?

The answer to this question is important ; but it is not difficult. Indeed, it is questionable whether a single reader has not by this time supplied the answer. Officers and men—especially those of the 92nd—fought as nobly as ever soldiers had done on battlefield. They fought with that dogged determination which has rarely failed to bring triumph to British arms, yet the result was deplorable, overwhelming disaster. And this disaster was due, not to any mischance, not to any unforeseen contingency arising to invite reverse ; but to the fact that victory was from the first an impossibility under the conditions by which it was sought—a handful of men were asked to hold a position for "three days," which could not be maintained for as many hours, and from which the Boer thousands should have driven them in half the time they took. The force was exposed to certain defeat without its commander having used any of the means available to minimise the risk. Indeed, as General Hay proves, he suicidally invited combat by ordering, or permitting, the firing which revealed his presence to the enemy. He is dead—he died with the many others whose lives were sacrificed, and his object and intentions can never be fully known. But on the face of it, the seizing of Majuba in the manner he did seems, in the absence of his reasons, a purposeless and insane movement — a blunder of a disastrous and inexcusable kind. He had, it is known, been urged, in absence of General Wood, to seize his opportunity to make a reputation. What share, if any, the letter we spoke of in another chapter as having been found on his body after death may have had in impelling him to his course of action cannot even be surmised ; but, if it had any influence at all, it would only show how ill-fitted he was for his responsible position.

Major the Hon. J. Scott Napier's Statement.

On this point Major the Hon. J. Scott Napier writes in language as convincing as it is strong. The Major, who endorses the statement of General Hay and that contained in the 92nd Record, says he collected his information from independent sources, " both in our own camp, and from Boers who were present at the action." Major Napier then proceeds :—

" Although stationed some miles from Majuba Hill, I was able, with the aid of a telescope, to see some portion of the engagement, and I afterwards made a careful study of the ground and positions occupied. The disaster was the result of a series of inexcusable blunders in the art and practice of war. In the first place, there was nothing to gain and everything to lose by premature action. There was no question of the enemy being reinforced, taking the offensive, or even shifting their position ; while, on the other hand, General Colley's strength might have been doubled within twenty-four hours' notice by moving up troops from Newcastle. In fact, General Wood had himself gone down to Newcastle to bring up other regiments, and it was during his absence that the Majuba disaster occurred. Moreover, it was almost universally known and believed in camp that General Wood had desired that no offensive movement was to be undertaken by his second in command till his return. General Colley staked his all in occupying a position the extent and nature of which were unknown to him, while its distance from Lang's Nek deprived it of any value, it being out of rifle range of the Boer lines. The General had neglected to provide himself with mule guns, which might have been used from Majuba heights with good effect as a covering fire to an infantry attack from below. As it was, General Colley, after a hard and exhausting night march, found himself in an untenable position, with a handful of men composed of detachments of four distinct corps. He had actually lost his supports and separated himself from his reserve ammunition. When day came no systematic steps were taken either to hold the hill or effect a retreat, although he had four or five hours of daylight before an attack commenced."

Splendid Fighting Material.

" The material in the ranks from which General Colley selected his force," continues Major Napier, "was certainly the finest which could, even at that time, be supplied from the British infantry, and better trained, more experienced than would now be available. In my humble opinion it would be difficult to find in the records of our military disasters one where blame rested less on the shoulders of the rank and file, and more heavily on those of their leader, who was alone directly and personally responsible for the conception and failure of his plan." The Major adds—" The cowardly reflections cast on the rank and file of the 92nd are as unmerited as they are contemptible."

This is scathing criticism, but it is borne out by the narrative which we have now published. The blunder was Colley's, and his alone ; the disaster was the direct result of the blunder. No better fighting could have been performed than that of the officers and men engaged ; no possible efforts of such a handful could ever have been successful in the circumstances. The men were led up to Majuba top, as sheep to the shambles, and doomed to die the victims of the thousands of Boer marksmen invited to shoot them down.

The Honours Gained.

The honours of disaster sounds incongruous. Yet it is more difficult to bear oneself nobly in disaster than in victory ; and those who do so are doubly worthy of reward. Major Fraser was the senior effective officer left after the death of Colley, and his report forwarded through General Wood stated that " throughout the movement, and during the whole of the action, Commander Romilly, R.N. ; Major Hay, 92nd ; and Captain Morris, 58th Regiment, all gave the General unremitting support. The following were conspicuous for gallant conduct :—Lieutenant Hamilton, 92nd Regiment, and Lieutenant Lucy, 58th Regiment. Both were exposed to severe fire during seven hours. Lieutenants Wright and Macdonald, 92nd Regiment, behaved with the greatest coolness and courage, and to the last made every effort to turn the course of events. Captain Macgregor, 92nd Regiment, exposed himself constantly with the men of his regiment, in addition to performing his duties as *aide-de-camp*. . . . The conduct of the 92nd was excellent throughout ; many whose names I cannot recall or did not know behaved with coolness, and their shooting was uniformly steady."

General Sir E. Wood, in his despatch to the Secretary for War accompanying the above, said :—" I feel confidence in submitting for favourable consideration the names of those mentioned in the report. To what has been adduced in that report with regard to the conduct of Captain Macgregor, 92nd Highlanders, I would in addition bear testimony to the activity he displayed during the march up-country, conduct which induced me to recommend him to Sir George Colley, who subsequently informed me that he had decided to appoint Captain Macgregor to his staff as *aide-de-camp*. From independent sources I have heard much of the conspicuous gallantry displayed by Lieutenant Lucy, 58th Regiment ; by Lieutenant Hamilton and Second Lieutenant Macdonald, 92nd Highlanders ; by Corporal Farmer, Army Hospital Corps ; and by No. 1865, Private John Murray, 92nd Highlanders. I recommend Corporal Farmer for favourable consideration for the Victoria Cross, and Private Murray for the distinguished service medal."

And there the " honours" end. We have not heard that the Cross or the medal was ever bestowed. And the officers who had fought so bravely got nothing but the empty distinction of being "mentioned in despatches." But they possessed the best of all honours, the consciousness of having done their duty.

Thus has the story of Majuba been told, not in all

its details, but more fully than ever it has been before. It has been told, too, by men who passed through the crisis, and who have declared what they saw, what they did, and how and why they did it.   There can be but one conclusion in the mind of the reader :—That whosoever blundered, the officers and men detailed for the duty of defending Majuba fought as became true British soldiers, and that, if there was wavering anywhere, it was not in the ranks of the Gordon Highlanders, who braved the murderous Boer fire till five-sixths of their .number lay killed and wounded on the field.   They proved themselves, as at Charasiah and Candahar, worthy upholders of the prestige which this corps had gained on many a bloody field, and supported the best traditions handed down from the immortal heroes of the long series of victories which culminated at Quatre Bras and Waterloo.

THE END.